Divorced
But
Still My Parents

Divorced But Still My Parents

Shirley Thomas, Ph.D.

and

Dorothy Rankin

Illustrations by Holliday Thompson

ACKNOWLEDGEMENTS

Shirley Thomas would like to thank the thousands of boys and girls who have taught her about children and divorce. She also thanks her sister, Amy Nickell, for her editorial contributions, and her family's very special long-time friend, Patches.

Dorothy Rankin thanks her children, Nathan and Ariel, who continually awe and inspire her, and her good friend Holli Thompson, whose illustrations make Kristen's story come alive.

Springboard
Publications

3rd Printing 2005

Printed in the USA

ISBN 0-9646378-5-5

Library of Congress 97-091848

Contents

Appendix

THE STAGES OF GRIEF IN CHILDREN

Children experience loss and pain at least as much as parents when divorce changes the family. They have lost the intact family and must adapt to major differences in how they live. As boys and girls go through family separation, nothing we do can prevent their stark realization that mother and father will no longer be together.

This book is written to help children with their reactions to divorce. Parents can also help by reading the book along with their children.

Divorced But Still My Parents is organized according to the five stages of grief first outlined by Elisabeth Kübler-Ross in her studies about human reaction to death. Dr. Ross identified phases of mourning that follow whenever permanent loss occurs. When children lose their families of origin through divorce, they go through the grieving process along with their parents.

Though there are differences between loss of the original family and loss of a loved one through death, the stages of adjustment are the same.

Stage 1   DENIAL *Children don't want divorce.* Boys and girls may refuse to accept the loss. They deny that the separation is happening or insist the parents will reunite.

Stage 2   ANGER *Divorce makes people angry.* Children often experience resentment or hostility. They may become angry at one or both parents, at brothers, sisters, friends, or even at themselves.

Stage 3   BARGAINING *Some children try to stop divorce.* They make efforts to postpone the loss or try to manipulate the parents by changing their own behavior.

Stage 4   DEPRESSION *Kids feel sad and lonely and scared.* Sadness about the permanence of the loss is normal. Many other negative feelings must also be worked through.

Stage 5   ACCEPTANCE *Children feel better before long.* They gain a more peaceful understanding as time goes on. When boys and girls become comfortable with their new lives, they can once again feel the joy of childhood without the burden of grief.

Children cannot achieve a lasting acceptance of their parents' divorce without working through the painful stages of grief. Like adults, they process each feeling at a pace they can handle, moving on to the next stage when they are ready. The important thing is for parents and children to allow themselves to grieve, so they can move beyond the divorce.

This book will lead your child through the five stages of grief in a gentle and supportive way. Each phase is explained in words children in the middle years of childhood can understand. The most common problems and worries faced by boys and girls are included, along with ideas for coping and feeling better.

The story of Kristen is a central part of *Divorced But Still My Parents*. Stories are wonderful vehicles to communicate important and difficult concepts to children. By imagining Kristen's experience, they see that they are able to cope with their feelings. They will gain confidence and, through the process of identification, learn that if Kristen can get through divorce, they can too.

How to Use This Book

Boys and girls under the age of nine usually benefit from having a parent or counselor read *Divorced But Still My Parents* with them. Young children feel more secure and less troubled reading about divorce issues in the company of an understanding adult. You can encourage your child to complete the activities and drawings in the way that feels most natural, even using colored pencils or crayons to be more expressive.

Many older children will prefer to read *Divorced But Still My Parents* on their own. Using this book more personally as a journal, these children profit from recording their feelings privately. Some of them will grow to treasure their own drawings and written expressions as an intimate log of how they worked through the family separation.

Tell your child that *Divorced But Still My Parents* is his or her own book for helping with feelings about divorce. Ask if the child wishes to have you read along and encourage your son or daughter to go through all the chapters from beginning to end.

An Important Note

Research on divorce shows that children can grow up to be happy and well adjusted even with their parents living apart. The critical factor is how parents react themselves and how well they deal with their own grief responses. When adults struggle with their own divorce acceptance for too long, their children do too.

Mothers and fathers who accept the reality of divorce without perpetuating anger and blame make it possible for their children to go on with normal tasks of childhood. Children suffer most when parents fail to let go and continue the state of conflict.

The major burden of helping children with divorce is always on the adults rather than on the children. The better you and your former spouse do to recover from divorce yourselves, the better your children will do.

THIS BOOK BELONGS TO

_____

A MESSAGE TO KIDS

If your mom and dad are divorced, or if they are getting a divorce, reading this book will help. By going through the chapters, you will learn about problems all kids have when their parents decide to live apart. You will see how to handle your feelings and you will start to feel better.

You can read this book all at once, or slowly, just a few pages at a time. There are places for you to write your ideas and to draw pictures of yourself with your family.

Inside this book is a story about Kristen, a kitten whose parents are going to divorce. As you follow Kristen through her new living adventure, you will feel better about coping with changes in your own family.

You can read and work in this book by yourself or ask your mom or dad to read with you. However you choose to do it, GO FOR IT! This book is yours.

We care about you.

Shirley Thomas and Dorothy Rankin
The Authors

WHAT IS A FAMILY?

A family begins when a man and woman get married. They create a home together because they are in love and want to share their lives. The husband and wife are the first members of the family.

Babies are born when a man and woman decide to have a child. They create a baby that grows in the mother's womb until the child is born. So whenever a baby boy or girl comes into the world, he or she has two biological parents.

Many times the mother and father decide to have more than one child because they want a larger family. Some parents adopt girls or boys whose birth parents cannot take care of them. Adopted children are special because they were chosen by Moms and Dads who love them simply because they were born. Brothers and sisters, whether adopted or not, grow to love each other as much as their parents love them.

Families live together in a home and do lots of things as a group. The mom and dad are always in charge, and they are responsible for the children. Parents decide where the family will live, where the children will go to school, and how to earn money for food and clothes. The parents' job is to protect and take care of children as they grow.

Families are wonderful because everyone loves one another. Parents teach kids about life, and help them learn to solve problems. They encourage kids to make friends and develop their talents. Children and parents have fun going places and doing things together.

Adults and children who live in families feel safe and happy in their homes. They work and play alongside each other and give each other love.

Your family is made of you and the parents who cared for you from the time you were very little. Your family may have other children or you may be the only child.

DRAW A PICTURE OF YOU WITH YOUR FAMILY WHEN YOU WERE VERY LITTLE

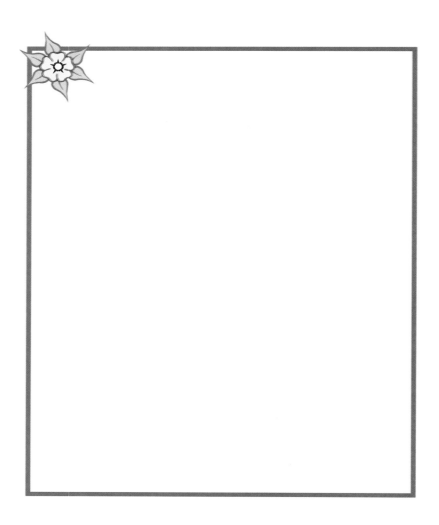

WHAT IS DIVORCE?

Sometimes problems develop for moms and dads who are married.

As time goes on, parents change, but they don't always change in the same way. Then they may disagree, become unhappy, and may argue or fight. Although they will always love their children, sometimes parents stop loving each other.

Parents who are very unhappy decide to live apart so they can be happy again. They ask the court for a DIVORCE,* and set up different homes. They talk about where the children will live and how to best take care of their boys and girls.

Children never cause divorce, though some kids think they do. Marriage and divorce are for parents only, and when parents divorce, they still love the children very much. They simply must separate in order to be happy themselves.

Most kids have two homes after divorce — one with Mom and one with Dad. Children usually spend time

* This and other important words can be found in the Divorce Dictionary at the back of this book.

with each of their parents. In a way, the world seems bigger after divorce because kids have more places to go.

There are many kinds of families with separated parents, and not all children have two homes. Some boys and girls have just one parent with one child and only one home to live in. Others have step-parents and step-brothers and sisters who move into one house or the other. You may live with your grandparent, another relative, or a foster parent, and these people are your family too.

Divorce means that families change, but your mom and dad are your parents forever. Both of them will keep loving you as days and weeks go by, and other adults will love you too. Even when children grow up with divorce from the time they are very little, they learn that both parents will always believe they are special.

Your family will have a different form after your parents divorce. But you and your parents are STILL a family and you will always be loved.

THINK ABOUT YOUR FAMILY

Which parent do you live with now?

When do you spend time with your other parent?

Who else is in your family?

Write your dad's address and phone number here.

Write your mom's address and phone number here.

What do you like about your family?

If you could change something about your family, what would it be?

DRAW YOURSELF WITH YOUR FATHER HERE

Things I like to do with my dad:

_____

_____

_____

DRAW YOURSELF WITH YOUR MOTHER HERE

Things I like to do with my mom:

_____

_____

_____

KRISTEN'S STORY

Part 1

A World Turned Around

"I am so-o-o happy!" thought Kristen. Sitting between her parents in the deep grasses, she pretended to listen carefully with them for field mice. Her father, his ears pricked upward and neck stretched, was trying to pick out movement in the grass. Her mother gave Kristen a little lick near her whiskers. Hunting for mice was serious business, and Kristen was supposed to be learning how.

Kristen was a very clever and very pretty little kitten. Her coat was a glossy yellow-orange and her socks were white. But her most unusual feature was her striped tail, which made her feel like a tiger.

Not only was Kristen clever and pretty, but she was, indeed, a very happy kitten. She had everything she wanted. On the farm where she lived, she had many friends. Her mother and father loved her, and she spent a lot of time with each of them. She and her father would play outside, exploring the life around them, wrestling and tickling each other in the sun. Her mother would lie down beside her in the barn, grooming her and telling her stories. Kristen's world seemed just about perfect.

But then one day, something happened to change all that. When Kristen thought about it later, she figured she should have seen it coming. Because, although both her parents spent time with Kristen, they had been spending less

and less time with each other. Then finally, on what seemed like the darkest day of her life, they gave her the news that would change her world forever.

"Your father and I have decided to get a divorce," said her mother. "We feel we just can't live together anymore."

"I know it hurts now," said her father, "but things will get better, you'll see."

Kristen was stunned and silent. She looked at them both in disbelief. How could this be happening? Surely her parents, who could fix just about anything, could fix their own marriage!

At last Kristen stood up and cried out, "But you can't do this. It's not fair! It's just not fair!" Sobbing, she ran into her room and slammed the door. But her parents had not yet finished all they had to say. More bad news was still to come.

* * *

The sun was creeping down behind the fence. Kristen and her parents had just finished a sad and silent dinner. The tension was very thick, and Kristen felt utterly miserable. Her mom and dad each spoke to her but not to each other.

Finally, her mother said, "Kristen, I'm moving to the city, and I want you to come with me, at least for part of the time. The rest of the time you'll live here with your daddy. We'll take some of your toys and things to our new apartment and leave the rest of your belongings here in the country."

The tone of her voice told Kristen there could be no discussion—no argument. The decision had been made, and Kristen would have to go along with it.

After helping to clean up, Kristen walked outside. The barn stood nearby, and coming from it were the familiar smells of all her animal friends. She needed to talk to someone—someone who would understand.

Kristen had known Rachel all her life. Rachel was an old and wise raccoon, and Kristen knew that if she had to leave the farm she'd miss Rachel the most. She didn't know exactly where Rachel lived, but she often saw her by the trash bins outside the house. Rachel was very generous with what she found there and often gave Kristen the best morsels.

"Rachel!" cried Kristen as she turned the corner of the house. "You there?"

"Sure I'm here, sweetie. Just got back this afternoon." She looked Kristen over. "Something troubling you, dear?"

Kristen hardly knew what to say. She walked twice in a circle and sat down. "Everything's falling apart and I can't do a thing about it. My mom and dad say they are getting a divorce. And as if that isn't bad enough, Mom is moving to the city, and I'm supposed to live there with her part of the time. I hate the city."

"Is that so!" said Rachel, slowly and thoughtfully. This wasn't quite the response Kristen was expecting. She waited, for Rachel often took her time considering her words. Usually it was worth the wait.

"Ever been to the city?" she finally asked.

"Well, no," said Kristen. "But I know I don't like it."

Rachel looked up at the stars filling the night sky and sighed. "Seems like your mom doesn't much like it here, honey bunch," she said.

"Well I don't see why not," said Kristen. "In fact, I'll bet that after she's in the city a while we'll move back. Maybe Mom just needs a vacation.

"You know what I'm going to do?" she continued. "I'm going to hide when it's time to go. Mom will have to go there by herself and then she'll come back for good because she'll miss us so much."

"Kristen, honey, I don't know if that plan is goin' to work. Let me give you a little advice. Don't worry so much about your parents right now. The thing to do is take care of yourself. Know that no matter what, your parents will always be your parents and will always love you. Just take one day at a time.

"You know, this move to the city could be kinda' fun. Think of it as an adventure! You're sure to meet some new friends. And you know I'll always be here for you." With that, Rachel jumped down from the garbage can, gave Kristen a little nuzzle on her neck, and disappeared into the nearby woods.

To be continued

17

CHILDREN DON'T WANT DIVORCE

ust like Kristen, children usually don't want divorce to happen at first. Kids like to have things stay the same as they have always been, and they don't want their families to change.

When you first learned about your parents' divorce, you may have started to cry. Maybe you hated the word *divorce* and pretended you couldn't hear what your Mom and Dad were saying. Some kids even put their hands over their ears and yell out that their parents have to stay together. Others try to be grown up and act like it doesn't matter at all, but inside they are frightened and worried.

Kristen didn't want divorce because she didn't want things to change. She was scared and angry about having to move from the country to the city because her parents did not give her a choice. She thought the only good life was the one she had always known.

When Rachel pointed out that Kristen's new way of life could be fun and interesting, she helped her little friend see that divorce is not all bad. With Rachel's help, Kristen started to realize that living sometimes in the city and sometimes in the country might be exciting. Later on we will also find that, though Kristen misses her father when she goes to the city, she feels better the minute they are together again.

When *your* mom and dad have lived apart for a while, you will probably start to like your new life too. Like Kristen, you will find that having two homes can be OK or even better than before because now Mom and Dad don't argue and everyone can be happier.

Kids have different lives after Mom and Dad divorce. Your parents live in separate places, but they are still your parents and always will be.

DRAW YOUR MOM'S HOUSE
AND YOUR DAD'S HOUSE

LIST OF SAME AND DIFFERENT

After divorce, some things are the same as they have always been, though there are many changes.

Things that are the **SAME**   •   **Things that are** *different*

1. *I still have Mom and Dad.*   •   1. *Mom and Dad live apart.*

2. *I still have to follow rules.*   •   2. *Mom and Dad can't live together.*

3. *I have to do my chores*   •   3. *My chores are different in each home.*

4. *Mom and Dad still love me.*   •   4. *There are different rules in each home.*

SAME

CAN YOU ADD TO THE LISTS?

DIFFERENT

5._____   •   5._____

6._____   •   6._____

7._____   •   7._____

KRISTEN'S STORY

Part 2

Anger and Other Bad Feelings

"How do you like it, dear?" asked Kristen's mother. They were standing on a balcony, looking over the big city. Millions of lights glowed around them from other buildings near and far. Kristen had never seen anything like it. Their apartment was on the fourth floor. Although the view was breathtaking, Kristen missed the sweet smells the country. She was still angry with her mother and didn't answer her. Instead, she walked inside.

"We have to talk about this, you know," said her mother following closely behind. "What is really wrong?"

"I miss Daddy," said Kristen, "that's what is wrong. I miss a lot of things. I don't like it here. And I don't like you." And with that, she put

her tail straight up in the air, spit and hissed at her mother, and walked away.

"Kristen, don't you act that way while we're talking," said her mother. "You've got to tell me how you feel, not behave in a crude, ill-mannered way." But Kristen kept going. She walked right under a bed, curled up in a corner, and didn't come out all night.

The next morning, Kristen's mother went straight into Kristen's room. "We've got to talk about the way you acted last night. In this house, we don't walk away from each other while we're dealing with problems. It's rude and I won't have it.

"Being angry doesn't give you an excuse to act any way you please, and it hurt me when you spit at me like a wild cat. You're just going to have to figure out some other way to deal with your anger."

Though her body remained stiff and curled up in a ball, Kristen opened one eye to listen.

"I know you miss your dad," her mother continued. "Why don't you draw him a picture? Draw a picture of your new bedroom, and you can take it to him when you see him."

After a while, Kristen got up and drew a picture of her new room. Then she drew a picture of herself and her mom and dad together back on the farm. After staring at it for a long time, she grabbed a black crayon and angrily marked all through it. Kristen scratched the paper in anger, and her tears fell on the drawing, smearing all the colors together.

* * *

Sometime later, when Kristen was sitting in front of her apartment watching all the cars and people and general busyness all around, she heard a very familiar voice.

"So? How do you like your new place?"

It was Rachel!! She was hiding behind, what else, a trash can.

"Rachel! What are you doing here?" Kristen could hardly believe her eyes.

"I come here lots of times, Sweetie. In fact, your new neighborhood happens to be one of my favorite vacation spots."

"But you never told me you went to the city. How come you never talked to me about it?"

"Well I figured you'd go an' ask me all kinds of questions 'bout it, and I wanted you to see it for yourself. So? What do you think?"

"I don't know," said Kristen. "It's kind of OK. But I wish things were like they used to be."

Rachel licked her paws for a while, casually eying the cars speeding by. Kristen was used to these silences.

"Miss your daddy?" Rachel asked.

"Yeah, I miss him."

"Ever going to see him again?"

"Sure, I'm going to see him again. Day after tomorrow!"

"So while you're here, enjoy what's here. And when you go back to the farm, enjoy what is there!"

Rachel stuck her nose in the can and pulled out half a bologna sandwich. She took out the meat and gave it to Kristen.

"So, did you meet Coty?" Rachel asked, glancing over her shoulder at a first-floor apartment window. A planter just outside the window was crammed with daisies and daffodils, giving a cheerful look to the entire building.

"Apartment 3b. Nice kid. But you can't go talking to him while you're still so angry. You wouldn't make a good impression."

"I can't help it, Rachel. I'm so mad I could spit."

"You know what I do when I'm mad?" asked Rachel. "First I go to a special, secret place. A place that's all my own. Then I start thinking about other things. I don't mean about how

27

things should be different. I mean OTHER things — things that have nothing to do with what is happening around me. Like I think about the ocean sometimes. Or I think about the tea parties my grandma used to have. Or I think about that stupid horse Fred and the way he chews his food. Or I think about what new adventure I'll make for myself tomorrow. Or I think about...."

"OK, OK," shouted Kristen. "I'll think about it!"

When Rachel had gone, Kristen jumped up onto the planter and hid among the flowers to get a look inside. Sitting under a piano was a little gray kitten. He was studying the shiny pedals and was about to pounce when he suddenly spotted Kristen. As they stared curiously at one another, little did Kristen and Coty know that they would soon be the best of friends.

To be continued

28

DIVORCE MAKES PEOPLE ANGRY

hen kids find out that Moms and Dads have decided to live apart, lots of them get angry, like Kristen. Children get mad because they miss having Mom and Dad both at home together, and there is no way to make things be the same as they used to be. The parents' decisions are final, and kids are not in charge.

It may seem strange that even though parents separate so they can be happier, for awhile they still seem angry and unhappy. Parents also have to do things in new ways when they divorce, and this can make them upset. In Part 3 of Kristen's story, we will see that when her father acts grouchy and irritable, she thinks it might be because of her. But the father is just worrying about his own problems, and Kristen has to worry about hers.

After divorce, parents may be angry for lots of reasons. Some may have to go to work and stay away from home longer than they really want. Others may have trouble handling all the laundry, cleaning, and shopping because they have to work all day, too. Parents get grumpy and sometimes lose their tempers when they have so much to do.

Like adults, kids get mad about many things after divorce because life is not the same as it was. Some kids live in one home with only one parent taking care of them, and they don't like having so many chores. Children who live in two homes often get mad about having to go back and forth. Some kids have only a few changes to make, but others have to put up with lots of new things about life, and maybe you do too.

It's OK for grown-ups *and* children to be angry about divorce, but it is not OK for anyone to show angry feelings in ways that can make things worse. For example, we should not punch, kick, scream, or yell. These actions only make people angrier, and things do not get better.

Angry feelings are normal, but angry actions don't make things the way you want them to be. So it is best for kids and grownups to try to get rid of angry thoughts and ideas about divorce.

Parents love their boys and girls, but they still get angry about divorce. Children love their moms and dads, but they still get mad about divorce, too.

ANGRY FEELINGS CHECKLIST

Check the things that made YOU angry after divorce:

- ☐ Not having Mom and Dad live together
- ☐ Having to change homes so often
- ☐ Mom and Dad still fighting
- ☐ Having too many chores
- ☐ Missing Mom or Dad
- ☐ Having to remember what to take to Dad's or Mom's
- ☐ Losing friends from my old neighborhood
- ☐ Going to a different school
- ☐ Moving to another home or city
- ☐ Not having things the way I want them

What else makes you angry?

- ☐ _____
- ☐ _____
- ☐ _____

WHAT TO DO ABOUT ANGER

Children must learn to cope with angry feelings after divorce. Anger is normal but can be dangerous. It's not OK to hurt people, things, or yourself when you feel angry.

There are lots of **SAFE** ways to make yourself feel better.

Talk to Yourself

Say these things to yourself so you can stay in control:

It's OK to be angry about divorce.

I can control my angry feelings.

It's normal to be mad about divorce.

I can *say* I am angry.

I can work out my anger safely.

I can draw pictures of my angry feelings.

What else can you say to yourself?

_____

DRAW OR SCRIBBLE YOUR ANGRY FEELINGS ABOUT DIVORCE

Getting them out on paper will help.

Help Yourself With
ABC

Learn these ABCs to feel better about
your parents' divorce.

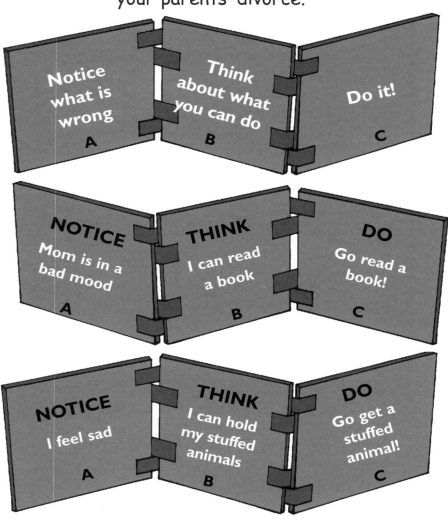

Two More Good Ideas

Everybody has angry feelings, but nobody ever likes them. Here is what you can do when you feel mad.

Breath deep.

Close your eyes. Breath in and pretend you are filling up your body with air. Fill yourself up from the very bottom of your feet to the very top of your head. Then breathe out again slowly, like you are squeezing all the air out of a balloon. Breathing deep will calm you down, and you will be less angry.

Think of a happy picture.

Close your eyes. Pretend you can see a picture in your head, of something that makes you happy. Imagine a place you love to see, like a beautiful forest, or the ocean, or a happy playground with kids having fun. Think about being there yourself, and you will start to feel relaxed.

DRAW YOUR HAPPY PICTURE HERE

KRISTEN'S STORY

Part 3

What to Fix and Who to Blame

The day soon came when Kristen was walking back with her mother to the country. She couldn't wait to see everyone, especially her dad. As she approached the farm, she saw him waiting by the house.

"Come on, Mom. There's Daddy! Hurry up."

"Wait, Kristen. I'm going to say good-bye right here."

"But why? Can't you just come in for a while? Let's all spend some time together. You can go back to your apartment tomorrow, or maybe you'll decide to stay even longer."

"No, I can't, honey. Your father and I have made our final decision; we are going to live apart, and that's that. Now give me a kiss. I'll be thinking about you. But I know you'll have a good time here with your dad. Remember, you can call me any time you feel like it." With that, she gave Kristen several licks all over her face, then turned and walked away.

Kristen watched her mother leaving, then looked back at her father. For a moment, she couldn't move because she felt so torn. In her dreams, she had pictured bringing her parents back together at the farm, where they would all live and be happy forever and ever. But this joyous moment had now turned sour.

"Hey, Furball." That was her dad's pet name for her, and it always made her feel warm inside. "Come on inside and I'll fix you some milk."

* * *

The time Kristen spent with her father went quickly. In some ways, it was just as before, and at times Kristen felt very happy. Father and daughter wrestled around on the floor and went exploring in the nearby woods. They chased mice together and cuddled in the evening. But still there was something different about her dad. He often seemed quiet and distracted—as if he were thinking about something far away.

The second day she was there, Kristen roamed around the farm, visiting all her friends. For a long time she talked with Alice, her spider friend, about the hows and whys of making of a spider web. So fascinated was Kristen with Alice's stories that she forgot about her father's problems. Kristen found herself purring with happiness.

When she suddenly realized she had lost track of the time and would be late for dinner, she said in a flurry, "Have to run home, Alice. See you later."

As she raced into the door, she couldn't wait to tell her father what she had learned.

"Guess why spiders make webs, Daddy!"

"To catch flies, of course," her father replied in an irritated voice. "Why are you coming in so late for dinner? You know I have rules about dinner time, and I expect you to follow them. Now sit down and eat."

Kristen felt terrible. She had been having a wonderful time with Alice while her father was here all alone. It must be her fault that her dad seemed so mad and so sad. She promised herself to do better: to never be late, to never leave her dad's side, to pay strict attention to the rules. Kristen was afraid that if he stayed angry at her, maybe her father wouldn't want her to come back!

After dinner, Kristen went right to the barn and to bed. She slept all that night and half the next day. What was the point of getting up, anyway. Nothing would ever be the same, and there was nothing she could do about it. When she was with her father, Kristen missed her mother, and when she was with her mother, she missed her father. Kristen got up, walked around in a couple circles, and curled back up in a ball. Soon she was asleep again.

* * *

"**Y**ou goin' to sleep your whole life away, child?"

Kristen picked up her head and opened one eye. There was Rachel, sitting on top of Rebecca, the cow.

"I don't see why not."

Rachel jumped down off the cow and sat by Kristen. "You want to talk about it, honey?"

"No, I don't want to talk about it," said Kristen.

"Well, you better talk about it. 'Cause if you don't, those feelings inside you are going to go all rotten and you'll get a bad stomach ache, which will give you something else to feel bad about. Then you'll stop eating and get skinny and Coty won't even know who you are when you get back to your mother's, and you'll have even more to feel bad about. This could go on and on forever!

"So, talk to me," demanded Rachel.

"I don't know, Rachel. I guess I'm just scared. If things can change so much, maybe they'll change even more. If Daddy gets mad at me, maybe he'll divorce me, too. I don't understand any of this. Why did they have to do this to me?

"And, besides, it's embarrassing. Jenny the sheep asked me where my mom is, and I told her she was on a little vacation. I didn't want to tell her what is really happening. The whole situation just stinks, and I figure if I just sleep for a few months, when I wake up, everything will be like it was."

"There's one thing you have to understand, child," said Rachel. "The divorce is going to happen, but the love a parent feels for a child is very, very special. It's unique — different in every way. Love like that is … *sticky*. No matter what you do, the love is stuck to you. No matter where you go, it just clings like fly paper. Can be rather annoying sometimes, but usually kids are happy to have it around. Seems it's always there when we most need it."

Rachel and Kristen talked long into the night. Kristen began to see that her parents' lives belonged to them, and her life belonged to her. Nothing she could do would change things, and even if she made mistakes her parents were still going to love her.

In the morning, Kristen felt much better. Breakfast with her dad was extra nice, partly because Kristen was hungry after her long sleep and partly because she was able to sense from her father that sticky kind of love Rachel had talked about.

To be continued

42

SOME CHILDREN TRY TO STOP DIVORCE

nly a few kids *want* their mom and dad to live apart. Even when parents argue and fight, most children want the family to stay together. But divorce is the grown-ups' decision and you have to let it happen.

Some children just wish their parents would get back together. Others try very hard to get their mothers and fathers to talk to each other in hopes that things will work out. Most girls and boys dream about how nice things used to be when Mom and Dad lived in the same house. Once in a while, they even wish they could be babies again so they could have two parents take care of them.

Kristen thought the divorce was her fault when her father became angry with her for coming home late. Then she tried to act perfect so her Dad would feel better and not blame her as much. With the way things had become, Kristen wasn't certain that her father would always love her.

Children often feel they cause divorce, even though adults have told them they are not to blame. They do their chores promptly, act extra nice, and try to be very helpful. But if you are hoping that Mom and Dad will get back together simply because of your good behavior, you will probably be disappointed even more.

Divorce is a grown-up problem, and when parents have ended their marriage, the family will be different forever.

Kristen will soon find out that her father very much wants her to keep coming to the farm to spend time with him. He loves her deeply, just as he always has. And your parents love you too.

Children cannot fix the family by getting their parents back together. Kids have to cope with changes when the parents have decided to divorce.

DOs AND DON'Ts ABOUT DIVORCE

DO

Accept change in your family.

Act your age.

Help with chores.

Ask questions.

Tell your Mom and Dad you love them.

Talk about your angry feelings.

DON'T

Try to get your parents back together.

Try to be grown up or act like a baby.

Try to be perfect and do all of Mom's or Dad's job.

Keep your feelings inside.

Take sides and think that one parent is bad, while the other is good.

Take your feelings out on someone else.

Can you add to these lists?

_____

_____

_____

_____

_____

_____

WRITE A LETTER TO YOUR PARENTS

Even though you can't stop divorce, you may wish you could. You have a right to all your feelings. It will help to tell your parents how you feel in a letter.

Dear Mom and Dad,

_____

_____

_____

_____

_____

_____

_____

_____

_____

_____

Love,

_____

THE STORY OF KRISTEN

Part 4

The Complete Strangeness of Things

The week was almost over. Today, Kristen's father seemed to be in a particularly good mood. "I'd like you to meet a friend of mine," he told her while they were walking in the field.

"O.K.," said Kristen. "What's his name?"

"Actually, *her* name is Cleo."

Just as he said this, a pretty brown striped cat ambled up to Kristen's father.

"So you're Kristen," she said. "It's very nice to finally meet you."

Looking at Cleo, then at her father, Kristen didn't know what to think. Except that this Cleo lady was standing too close to her dad.

But Kristen was taught to be polite, so she said hello and tried to smile. Maybe Cleo was her dad's friend, but Kristen would be happier if she would just keep her distance. This new development made Kristen very uncomfortable.

Cleo was clearly not going to keep her distance. In fact, she stayed with them all afternoon. She was nice, but Kristen had no private time with her father. The only good thing about Cleo's being there was that her father seemed happier. But this too bothered Kristen. Why couldn't her daddy be happy with just the two of them?

* * *

Back at her mother's, Kristen found many things to do. She and Coty became fast friends and would often play in the alley behind the apartment, looking for tasty morsels. Coty was living with his mother and stepfather, so he understood Kristen's feelings. They talked often, which always made Kristen feel good.

Kristen and her mother were getting along better. Once Kristen realized that her mother was absolutely positively staying in the city, Kristen began to see the apartment more as her own home too, not just as a place to visit. Just like on the farm, Kristen found her own secret private place—in the basement laundry room up on a high shelf.

After a while, Kristen got used to going back and forth. Sometimes bad things would happen, like her dad getting angry at her mother or her mother being upset about one thing or another.

She hated it most when her parents acted angry with each other and wouldn't talk to each other. Instead, they would give her messages to send back and forth. Like: "Tell your father I'm going to pick you up a little early on Monday." Or: "Tell your mother I don't appreciate being told what to feed you."

Rachel came to the rescue again, however. "Just don't do it anymore," she declared one winter morning. "Refuse to be the messenger! Tell them if they want to talk to each other they should leave you out of it. Tell them how it makes you feel. Parents just don't get it sometimes. But if you explain it, they'll understand."

Changing and learning new habits. These were the real challenges. Not only Kristen, but everyone in her family had to face them. They all had to adjust to many things about their lives—like how they talked to each other, how they scheduled things, how they managed their separate homes, and, perhaps most difficult, how they celebrated birthdays, holidays, and other special times.

As you will soon see, life on the farm went through some of the biggest changes for Kristen.

* * *

When Kristen next visited her father, Cleo was already there. So Kristen, who wanted as little to do with her dad's friend as possible, went off to visit her friends in the barn.

"How's it going, little one?" asked Rebecca the cow.

"Oh, fine." replied Kristen. "It's nice to be back. How are things around here?"

"Well, they're different. 'Course, things change all the time on a farm. You know how it is. The piglets are growing, a couple lambs were sold to the farmer down the road, that old rooster gets crankier every day, and the new kittens can be a real handfull. That little Fuzz seems to get into trouble all the time."

"What new kittens?" asked Kristen, eyes wide and startled. "And who's Fuzz? And what kind of name is that, anyway? *Fuzz!*"

"Oh, he's the youngun'. Kinda' cute, really. But he's ...."

Kristen didn't wait to hear the rest. She raced back to the house and found her father.

"Just who are these new kittens Rebecca is talking about, Dad? I didn't hear anything about new kittens."

"Sorry, kiddo. I was going to tell you tonight before they come over, but that Rebecca. Such a busybody. They're Cleo's children. I think you'll really like them. In fact, her little girl is right around your age."

"Wait a minute! I will NOT really like them. And it's not right that they're coming over here. Do they come here a lot? This is MY house. How come Cleo's kittens are over here?"

"Actually," said her father in that stearn voice of his, "this is *my* house. I share it with you. And now we're also going to share it with Cleo and her children.

"Please don't make this difficult, Kristen. This is the new life I've chosen, and I want you to be a part of it. You ARE a part of it. A big part. I know you'll like Cleo's family. But you have to give it a chance."

"Yeah? Well what if I don't want to be a part of it. I don't think I want a step-mother. Maybe I should just go live with Mom and forget about the farm. I don't want to intrude on your new family. This way we'll all be happier."

"That couldn't be further from the truth, Furball. I love you the same as always. I would be miserable if I couldn't spend time with you. Staying with just your mother isn't going to solve this problem because you need to have time with both of your parents.

"Tell you what," he continued. "Meet the kittens tonight, and tomorrow just you and I will go for a hunt together. Nobody else. We can talk it over again then."

To be continued

52

KIDS FEEL SAD AND LONELY AND SCARED

Remember when Kristen first learned her parents were going to divorce? She felt angry and didn't want it to happen. Many things seemed unfair, like having to move to a smaller home with her mom and making do without some of her things when she was with her dad.

Then Kristen began to experience other bad feelings, like being lonely and afraid things would never get better. Kristen felt especially sad when she missed her father while spending time with her mom in the city, even though she loved her mother very much.

Now Kristen is upset because her father has decided to go on with his life. The news that she will be getting new family members is shocking, and Kristen reacts with anger. But as we will see in Part 5, Kristen will learn to cope.

Sad or negative feelings happen to all children when their parents separate. You may be embarrassed when you have to tell your friends about the divorce, or you may worry about the future. Most kids are confused about the reasons for their parents' divorce. Even though your mom or dad may try to explain, it's hard to understand why parents would choose not to live together.

Children should not feel guilty about problems between their parents because divorce is never their fault. But you may feel ashamed of your parents, or humiliated, or feel that you have failed because you can't do anything about it.

It will help to remember that all children have at least some bad feelings, and it's normal for you to have them too. If you ask your friends whose moms and dads are divorced about *their* feelings, you will find you are not alone.

All kids have bad feelings and confusion about the future when their parents divorce. But there are many ways you can make yourself feel better.

Ways To Work Out Bad Feelings

1. Talk them away.

Find a parent, teacher or counselor who will listen to your feelings. Tell them about how angry or worried you are.

I can talk to _____

2. Write them away.

Start a journal or diary and write down how you feel each day. Soon you will see that you do not always feel bad, and you will feel better.

Write one idea here:

_____

_____

3. Play them away.

In a safe way, you can use dolls, action figures, and toys to play away your feelings. You can make up stories to act out for a friend or parent. You can even play *divorce*, and soon you will be less upset.

I can play with _____

FINDING THE BAD FEELINGS INSIDE

SAD

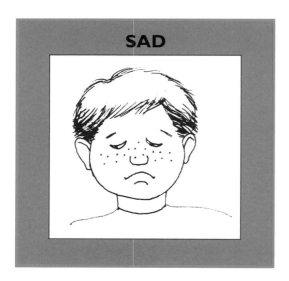

GUILTY

LONELY

CONFUSED

Think about when you have had these feelings.

AFRAID

ANGRY

ASHAMED

WORRIED

Talk about your feelings with your parents.

YOUR FIRST JOURNAL ENTRY

When you are alone, write more about how
you feel. You'll discover how writing about
your feelings can help.

Today's Date:

Journal Entry:

_____

_____

_____

_____

_____

_____

_____

_____

_____

_____

_____

NOTICE YOUR GOOD FEELINGS, TOO

While many things about divorce cause children to feel worried or sad, other things make them feel good. You will be free to smile again when your parents no longer argue or seem upset, and you will look forward to spending time in both of your homes.

If you move to a new city with your mom or your dad, you will feel *lucky* to make new friends and *glad* you can still write to your old ones. If your parents decide to live close to one another, you will be able to *enjoy* both your homes more often.

Once you and your parents have started to get used to your new routines, you will find yourself feeling *cheerful* and *lighthearted*.

KIDS HAVE THESE FEELINGS AFTER DIVORCE, TOO

RELIEVED

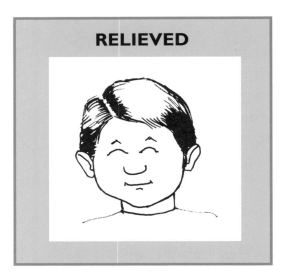

EXCITED

PEACEFUL

HAPPY

Have you ever felt these emotions since your parents separated?
These feelings are ok, too.

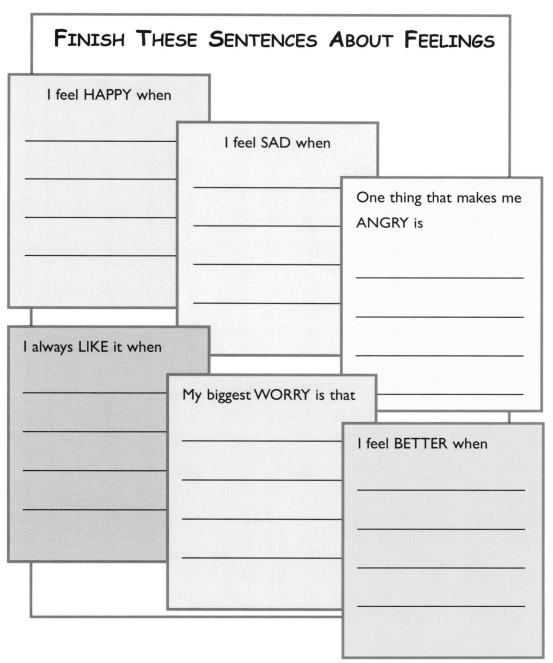

FINISH THESE SENTENCES ABOUT FEELINGS

I feel HAPPY when

_____

_____

_____

_____

I feel SAD when

_____

_____

_____

_____

One thing that makes me ANGRY is

_____

_____

_____

I always LIKE it when

_____

_____

_____

_____

My biggest WORRY is that

_____

_____

_____

_____

I feel BETTER when

_____

_____

_____

_____

THINKING GOOD THOUGHTS

Check off these thoughts as you read them out loud.
You can read them again anytime you want to
feel better about yourself and your family.

- ❑ I know my family cares about me.
- ❑ I know I am important.
- ❑ I am a special person.
- ❑ I can feel happy and good.
- ❑ I can do many things well.
- ❑ I know my mother loves me.
- ❑ I know my father loves me.
- ❑ I can accept the changes in my family.
- ❑ I like the way I am.
- ❑ I love both my parents.

Other people love me too. Some of them are . . .

_____

_____

_____

KRISTEN'S STORY

Part 5

Endings and Beginnings

Snow had been falling all day and was now piling up around the farm in large drifts. When the wind picked up, Kristen and her father nestled down in the utility shed to await their guests.

Kristen still wasn't happy. She decided she would simply get through this ordeal with Cleo and her children. She would speak as little as possible and go to bed early. Tomorrow she would go back to her mother's, and then decide what to do about her father. If she had

to be with Cleo's whole family in order to be with her father ... well, she would have to think that over. It seemed unlikely that it would ever work out.

At the sound of a soft meow, Kristen's dad opened the door of the utility shack. From the glow of the inside lights, Kristen could see three kittens standing in the snow with Cleo just behind. They all looked so cold and unhappy in the snow storm that Kristen couldn't help but want to welcome them in.

"Come in, come in!" said Kristen's father. Leo walked in first. The oldest of the children, Leo, was slim and gray, with black markings on his paws, chest and tail. He said "Hi" to Kristen, and she thought he gave her a little wink as he turned toward the rest of his family.

Next came Molly. She was around Kristen's age and kind of pretty. Her fur was long and fluffy and white, with orange and black markings.

Then Fuzz came running in. His mother must have been holding him back, for he sped into the room full speed, nearly crashing into the opposite wall. Fuzz was all black except for a spot of white just above his nose. Kristen had to admit, he was adorable.

Finally Cleo walked in and nuzzled Kristen's father. Kristen looked away at once, embarrassed. Then she noticed that Leo and Molly also seemed uncomfortable.

Dinner felt awkward. No one seemed to know what to talk about. But Fuzz kept everyone entertained. He was constantly moving and was much more interested in Kristen's tail than in dinner.

"What do you think?" whispered Molly after dinner as the two of them wandered away from the others.

"About what?" asked Kristen.

"About my mom and your dad," said Molly. "Kinda weird, isn't it?"

"Yeah," said Kristen, "Weird."

The two of them sat down on an old stuffed chair.

"But there is one good thing that might come out of all this," said Molly.

Kristen looked into Molly's eyes, and found they were kind and gentle.

"You see," she began, "there's something I've always wanted, all my life. And now, suddenly, I see I might get it."

"What is it, Molly? What have you always wanted?"

Molly looked down at the floor, then lifted her eyes, and said, "A sister."

* * *

"What do you think?" This time it was Kristen's dad asking that question. As promised, he was taking her out for a lone hunt. But they each had lost interest in hunting and instead took the opportunity to talk privately.

"I think I want more times like these, Daddy, with just you and me alone."

"I promise you, Furball, that will never stop. I will always make time for us together."

With a great relief, Kristen gave her dad a big hug, and her dad gave her a giant lick.

"I like Molly," Kristen said. "I never thought about it before, but it might be kind of fun having brothers and a sister."

"It sure will be different," said her father. "Leo is a really nice kid. And that Fuzz always makes me laugh."

"Maybe Molly and I can babysit!" said Kristen.

"Don't see why not.

"Kristen," began her father after a long silence, "there's something else we have to talk about. The holidays are coming up soon, and I know that's going to be a difficult time for you. Just because of all the changes, and the fact that you have two homes now."

Kristen didn't even want to think about that. What would the holidays be like without the family all together? Kristen loved the cozy and exciting feelings around this time of year, and she wanted always to feel them.

"I know it's hard to talk about," said Kristen's father as if reading her mind, "but it's better to set things up ahead of time so everyone knows what to expect.

"Your mom and I talked about this for a long time. We decided

that this year, you will spend Thanksgiving with your mother and Christmas with me. Next year, we'll do the opposite, Thanksgiving with me and Christmas with your mother."

This was tough. So many new ways of doing things! Kristen's world was still topsy-turvey, and she wondered if things would ever settle down.

"I guess that will be OK," she said. "But there is still one more thing I want to talk about. I don't know what to call Cleo. Is she supposed to be my mom or something?"

"Heavens no, Furball. Only your own mother will ever be your mother. Cleo will be more like an older friend or an aunt. And you can call her Cleo. She likes you a lot, you know."

"No, I didn't know. I guess I like her, too."

With that, the two of them walked back to the farm and talked about the weather and the rooster and the clever little mice they could never catch—just as they always had.

* * *

"Well, well, well, if it isn't my furry little friend!" It was Rachel. She was relaxing behind the apartment building munching on a carrot. "I don't see much of you these days. How're you doing?"

"Actually Rachel, I'm doing great! Molly and Leo have both become my very good friends. I kind of like being part of a big family. And then I like coming here and spending more quiet time with my mom. Sometimes life seems confusing, but mostly it's fun."

"That's my girl," smiled Rachel. "I knew you'd be alright if you just gave it some time. There are a lot of animals out there who love you.

What more could a kitten want?"

"Kristen dear! Time to come in and eat!" Kristen's mother was peering over the balcony through some potted flowers.

"Gotta go, Rachel. See you later?"

"I'll be around. The story ain't over yet, honey, if you know what I mean. And I'll always be here if you need me."

"Thanks, Rachel. So I'll see you around."

* * *

That night, Kristen and her mother curled up together in front of the fireplace, happy to be inside and warm.

"Sweetheart," her mother began, "I want to tell you how proud I am of you. Your father and I expected a lot from you, and we know it's been difficult at times. But you have really pulled through, and with flying colors."

"It isn't that things are any better or worse than they used to be before the divorce," said Kristen thoughtfully. "They're just different. *Real* different!"

"So true, Kristen. But one thing that will never ever change is the love your father and I both feel for you. Do you understand that?"

"Yes, I understand that," said Kristen.

And they slept curled up together the whole night through.

CHILDREN FEEL BETTER BEFORE LONG

Children are forced to learn new habits after their parents divorce, whether they want to or not. Did you notice how Kristen reacted with dismay at first when she learned she would be living in two places? Remember how she thought having a whole new family would be terrible? Even when kids don't like these different ways of life at first, they have to learn to live with them, because divorce is their parents' decision.

Like Kristen, most boys and girls find out they can feel good when their moms and dads live apart. They discover that even with all the changes and problems they encounter, life can be fun and interesting again.

By finishing this book, you are helping yourself learn to cope with your parents' divorce. You can help yourself even more if you think of life as an adventure. That way, no matter what kind of family or step-family your mom or dad decides to have, you will be able to be happy.

The most important thing for you to remember is that your mother and father will always love you. Even if you live alone with one parent and hardly ever see the other, or if you have the challenge of two big step-families to deal with, your parents will always believe you are very special.

Your mom and dad are your parents forever.

FEELING BETTER AGAIN

Say these things out loud to help yourself feel better:

It's normal to have bad feelings about divorce.

It's OK to feel sad, or mad, or to cry.

I am a very good child. The divorce is not my fault.

I can put my feelings into words and talk about them.

I know how to get rid of bad feelings.

I will feel happy again.

My parents are still my parents.

My fears will go away soon.

I will always love my parents.

My parents will always love me.

Choose one or two of these each day and say them out loud.
Say them just before you go to sleep or when you just wake up.

LIKING YOUR FAMILY NOW

List two good changes in your family since divorce.

1. _____

_____

2. _____

_____

SETTING GOALS FOR YOURSELF

You will help yourself by learning to set goals and working toward them. Your goal may be to save money, to make new friends, or to learn to like your step-family!

List some goals here:

1. _____

2. _____

3. _____

FAMILY PHOTO ALBUM

Tape or paste pictures of people you love on this page.

THINK ABOUT THE FUTURE

Draw a picture of the family you would
like to have some day!

Award

To

_____

**FOR MEETING THE CHALLENGES
OF YOUR FAMILY AND
FOR MAKING LIFE AN ADVENTURE.**

Congratulations on a job well done!

Write your name on the line, cut out the certificate, and keep forever.

Appendix

Great Questions and
Important Answers
for Kids

Divorce Dictionary

Great Questions and Important Answers for Kids

Q. How long is it going to take me to stop feeling sad about my parents' divorce?

A. Not as long as you might think. One thing you can do is talk to your parents often, and you will feel better before you know it.

Q. How can I keep track of going back and forth from my dad's house to my Mom's house?

A. Ask Mom or Dad for a calendar you can keep in your room. Write "Mom" on Mom's days and "Dad" on Dad's days. It's simple.

Q. If my Mom almost never calls or comes to see me, does she still love me?

A. Yes! Even when parents don't see their children, they have a special place for them in their hearts.

Q. Will I get a divorce someday?

A. Not if you don't want to. All grownups are different, and many stay together.

Q. Is it OK for me to have fun with my friends while Dad is feeling angry and unhappy?

A. Yes! You and your dad are different people. You should take care of yourself while your dad is solving his problems. Besides, your feeling better can help make your dad feel better too.

Q. What if I miss my Mom and I can't call on the phone?

A. Make a list of things to say when you can call or when you can write her a letter. Planning and writing things down will help.

Q. What should I do when I have a bad dream?

A. Tell your Mom or Dad about it. Then tell yourself things are fine and you can go back to sleep. Find a favorite doll or stuffed animal and put yourself back to bed.

Q. Will both my parents leave me if one has moved away?

A. No! When one of your parents leaves, the other will take care of you.

Q. My father never calls or comes to see me. Does that mean he doesn't love me?

A. No! It means your father has too many problems to demonstrate his love. Things may change someday.

Q. What should I do when Mom talks bad about Dad?

A. Tell her to stop! Tell her you love both your parents and it hurts you to hear her talk bad about Dad.

Q. What if Dad wants me to side with Him against Mom?

A. Tell him you won't side with him or your Mom either. Tell both your parents you love them because both are still your parents.

Q. What if Dad asks too many questions about Mom?

A. Tell him to stop! Tell him it is not your job to be "mailman" or deliver information about your Mom.

Q. What if I don't like Mom's or Dad's new friends?

A. Talk to your Mom or your Dad about it. You can work with your parents to learn to like their new friends more.

Q. Will my step-parent take the place of my Mom or my Dad?

A. Never! Your new step-mother or step-father will be another adult who cares about you, but will not replace your parent.

Q. Is it OK to love my new step-family?

A. Yes! You will find that you have enough love for everyone in your new family, including new brothers and sisters. Loving more people never takes away from the love you feel for family and old friends.

Divorce Dictionary

Attorney

Special person, sometimes called a lawyer, who helps parents with the laws about divorce. The attorney can go to court with Mom or Dad if necessary.

Child Support

Money that both parents contribute to take care of the children. The parent who does not live with the children most of the time pays the other parent his or her part of the money.

Court

Place where the judge makes the divorce legal and orders what is best for the children.

Co-Parenting

Divorced mothers and fathers still co-operate and work together to take care of their children.

Custody

Legal rule about which parent is responsible for making important decisions about the children. If both parents are equally responsible, they have *joint* custody.

Decree

Official document ending the marriage and outlining rules about how parents will take care of the children.

Divorce

Legal process parents go through to end an unhappy marriage.

Guardian ad litem

Special person — usually an attorney — picked by the court to help decide what is best for children when parents disagree.

Judge	Official person in court who makes divorce legal and sets up rules for taking care of the children when parents cannot agree.
Marriage	Legal agreement allowing a man and woman to live together as husband and wife.
Mediator	Special person hired by parents to help them make decisions about the family after divorce. Mediators help parents write down decisions to give to the judge.
Parenting Coordinator	Family specialist who helps parents learn to work together after divorce.
Parenting Plan	Rules or schedules for each parent to spend time with and care for the children. Children may live with one parent but may spend time in both homes.
Separation	The beginning of the legal divorce process, when a mother and father begin to live in separate homes.
Therapist	Special person, or *counselor*, who talks to parents and children about divorce. Therapists help everyone get over bad feelings and learn to cope with life after divorce.

YOUR SECOND JOURNAL ENTRY

Today's Date:

Journal Entry:

_____

_____

_____

_____

_____

_____

_____

_____

_____

_____

_____

_____

_____

_____

YOUR THIRD JOURNAL ENTRY

Today's Date:

Journal Entry:

_____

_____

_____

_____

_____

_____

_____

_____

_____

_____

_____

_____

YOUR FOURTH JOURNAL ENTRY

Today's Date:

Journal Entry:

_____

_____

_____

_____

_____

_____

_____

_____

_____

_____

_____

_____

_____

YOUR FIFTH JOURNAL ENTRY

Today's Date:

Journal Entry:

_____

_____

_____

_____

_____

_____

_____

_____

_____

_____

_____

_____